THE RETIREMENT RESCUE SYSTEM

"HOW TO NEVER RUN OUT OF MONEY IN RETIREMENT"

THE RETIREMENT RESCUE SYSTEM

"HOW TO NEVER RUN OUT OF MONEY IN RETIREMENT"

DAVID ABREU

The Retirement Rescue System

Copyright 2020 David Abreu

Cover by 99 designs

Printed in the USA

"I'm not afraid of storms,

for I'm learning how to sail my ship."

–Louisa May Alcott

TABLE OF CONTENTS

ACKNOWLEDGEMENTS

The information in this book was gathered from the wisdom and lifetimes of experienced professionals in the financial and insurance industry.

This industry is a tough one but a rewarding one, and a career path of love. You have to love people to want to help them. You have to love people to have tough conversations with them. We shine a light on life's obstacles that most people don't even want to acknowledge, let alone talk about.

However, personal and financial growth never comes from easy conversations but from tough ones. Conversations that make us look inward and think, take action and change course for the better. I want to thank everyone I have worked with in the past.

Thank you to the clients who allowed me to interview them for the content of this book and essentially making it possible to figure out mathematically-sound solutions to the obstacles that were in the way of their dreams and desired goals. This book would not exist without you.

Thank you to the insurance agents and career advisors who have made it their life's mission to educate retiree's everyday to make sure that their clients' finances are safe and secure — ensuring that nest eggs not only grow, but grow safely.

DISCLAIMER

Disclaimers are an important part of consumer protection in any industry, including the financial and insurance industry. With that being said, there are a few I would like to go through with you before you begin this book.

This publication contains the opinions and ideas of its author. It is intended to provide helpful and informative material on the subject matter covered. It is sold with the understanding that the author and publisher are not engaging or rendering professional services in this book. The information provided is not intended as tax, investment or legal advice, and should not be relied on as such. If the reader requires personalized assistance, you are encouraged to seek tax, investment, or legal advice from an independent professional advisor. The views expressed in this book are exclusively those of the author and do not represent the views of any other person or any company the author is associated with.

The author is not affiliated with the U.S. Government or any Government association.

This book has not been reviewed, approved, endorsed or authorized by any persons quoted in this book.

The material in this book is intended solely for information purposes. It should not be considered an offer of any product. One might use a variety of insurance products in planning for retirement, not only Fixed Index Annuities. The reader should consult with their own financial professional to assist them in making a decision on what is suitable and appropriate for them, based on their specific needs, age and timeline.

The reader needs to understand that the title of this book is just that – a book title. A catchy phrase used to attract readers. There is no promise to the reader that their retirement will be "rescued" in any way. It is up to the reader to research and directly seek a financial professional.

Any mention within this book of any particular product, strategy or system for specific retirement concerns is not to be construed as a definitive, only, or best available option for that purpose. For any given financial concern the reader has, there can be multiple solutions.

For ease of reading I may refer to financial professionals as agents, advisors, brokers, fee-based advisors, non-fee-based advisors, etc. In this I am not indicating who is or isn't licensed to sell these products. It is the reader's job to make sure the person or company you choose to work with is licensed to sell the product you want to purchase.

It is important to understand that a Fixed Index Annuity is not a security.

In this book I may reference the use of the RRS (Retirement Rescue System), or our system. This simply indicates the usage of a Fixed Index Annuity. Also, it is not our intention to give the full scope and details of an annuity, as there are many types of annuities available which are not discussed in this book. We do not set out the comparison of any products, as there are many investments that are available for one's specific situation. It is the reader's job to research and work with a professional, who can review all appropriate options available.

While reading this book I may use different terms to reflect the accumulation of money, like growth, gains, average growth rates, etc. Understand that I am referring to the interest credited, as interest credits are the only way Fixed Index Annuities grow in account or accumulated value. I intend to keep the conversation flowing by writing in conversational English and not financial or legal jargon. Terms used in this book similar to or related to the word "guarantee" or "guaranteed" describing an insurance product, including Fixed Index Annuities, are based on the fact that any contractual guarantees within the insurance policy are solely backed by the financial strength and claims-paying ability of the insurance company that offers the contract or policy. The contents in this book should not be taken as financial advice, or as an offer to buy or sell any securities, funds, or financial instruments. Any illustrations used or situations presented are hypothetical and are not necessarily specific to the reader's specific financial objectives. The contents of this book should not be taken as an endorsement or recommendation of any company or individual. Fixed indexed annuities are designed for long-term financial planning, and are not intended for short-term investment strategies. Guarantees or annuity payments may be subject to restrictions, fees, and surrender charges and as described in the annuity contract. Fixed Index Annuities are not stock market investments and are not in the stock or equity markets. Neither an index nor any market-indexed annuity is comparable to a direct investment in the equities market.

The author specifically disclaims any liability, loss, and risk, personal or otherwise, which is incurred as a consequence of any of the contents of this book. The author does not assume any responsibility for actions taken by the reader, and no one shall be entitled to a claim for detrimental reliance based on any information provided in this book. Use of any information provided in this book does not constitute a relationship between the reader and the author or his firm. No investment is risk-free. Every investment has some type of risk, whether its market risk, longevity risk, inflation risk or opportunity cost, or any other type of risks.

I hope this book gives you the value that I intended and can be a good starting point in your journey of financial understanding. Before making any decisions about your finances, it is best to have a detailed conversation with a licensed financial professional.

Wishing you and your family the best! Enjoy!

PREFACE

As the founder and CEO of a San Diego, CA-based financial and insurance services firm, a member and published author for the Forbes Finance Council, and someone who has power to change lives based on my knowledge and experience, I have been dreaming of writing this book for over 10 years and now I have finally made it happen.

The information I'm going to share with you in this book has helped millions of people just like you safeguard their retirements from risk of loss, given them inflation-beating rate of return averages and a beautiful stream of guaranteed lifetime income! I'm assuming that is what you are looking for as well, since you are reading this book.

Have patience and make it through to the end of this book and you will have more knowledge and power than 99% of the population. Take a highlighter and really dig into the chapters. Don't be intimidated. Believe in yourself. Take it all in because it's part of your financial journey, and I am so proud and honored to be your guide.

The result of executing the Retirement Rescue System is simple:

Safety, Growth and Income.

The trinity of retirement needs and wants.

- You'll have a predictable way to generate returns safely.

- You'll build a solid and safe foundation for your retirement savings.

- You'll get guarantees that your current retirement accounts don't offer.

- And you'll end up living a better life with less stress because everything will be organized and automatic to get you the best results possible!

Now before we get into the Retirement Rescue System we need to first understand the issues facing most retirees.

"Risk comes from not knowing what you're doing."

– Warren Buffett

PART 1

UNDERSTANDING THE PROBLEM

CHAPTER 1

CRISIS ON WALL STREET – DON'T BE A "JENNY"

Jenny's husband Steve picked up the morning papers. The headlines read: "Stocks Plunge"; "Market in Freefall"; Crisis on Wall Street".

He sighed and placed the newspapers on the hall table beside the grandfather clock – a feature of their middle-class home which had been passed down to him from his mother. The clock's relentless *tick, tock, tick, tock* seemed to add to the anxiety that hung in the air. A foreshadowing of time lost. Steve walked into the living room and turned on the news.

Jenny's heart was beating out of her chest as she struggled to remember the password to her 401k account. A sinking feeling of dread and despair came over her whole body as a wave of unwelcome fear. She felt like she had done something wrong, a sense of peril that could never be undone. The blaring news in the background turned into white noise as she stared at her 401k statement on her iPad with a sense of defeat. Her throat closed up and she began to feel her muscles tensing and her blood pressure increasing. As she stared frozen in terror, Jenny's 401k dropped, losing more than half of its value. Her eyes watered up as her mind immediately began to flashback through 30 years of work to get to where she was. Despair washed over her as she sat back in her chair.

Steve sat glued to the TV screen as the "Great Recession of 2008" reared its ugly head.

Tears rolled down Jenny's face as she stared at the screen with lifeless expression. She couldn't believe what was happening. She looked over at the grandfather clock, each second turning into a compounding loss. 30 years. She had given 30 years to this retirement plan. 30 years.

Jenny's real-life example

Jenny is 62 and she has $350k in her 401k. Her husband Steve is a 20-year-disabled vet with some medical issues. Jenny has worked at her job for 30 years and it's her time to retire. Every year she did what she thought needed to be done. She contributed to her retirement accounts, maxed out her 401k and made sure she was putting enough away. She made sure the bills were paid. She made sure they lived modestly to ensure their comfy retirement. She had an advisor through her HR Department that came once a year to the office where she works and spoke to the staff, but never had any type of relationship. It was more of a group thing. She just socked money away and forgot about it like she was told to do. In all normal circumstances, she was doing great.

Right before she retires the market crashed, the housing bubble bursts and the economy is in freefall. Her $350k she had saved for 30 years drops to $160k in a flash and continues to plummet. Her home value sinks and she's in panic mode. Her clear plans to retire are becoming blurry and seem unattainable. She knows she doesn't have enough to retire on and she's scared she'll lose everything. She's scared about the future.

She trusted her 401k would keep going up like her coworkers would often brag about. Jenny calls the brokerage firm's customer service number on her retirement account statement and is frantically asking questions. "What should I do?" she asks. "What are my options? I was supposed to retire this year."

Long and sad story short, she ends up drawing down on their remaining balance of her 401k because she needs the income to live on and her husband needed special care for his medical conditions.

When the markets started going back up over the years, she had spent most of the money on the mortgage, medical expenses and all of life's living expenses. Her 401k was her only income after she retired. Her kids had to pitch in every month to help with her expenses. She didn't plan properly, and she was living out the consequence of not paying close enough attention.

Jenny eventually had to pick up shifts at the nearby grocery store just to make ends meet. *How did this happen?* She thinks to herself. *Why now? Why at the end when life is supposed to be better? Why me? Why did this all happen?*

The sharp truth is this... No one is going to come to the rescue. No one is going to help you prepare if you aren't paying attention to what is happening around you and following a proven retirement system that is free from risk and loss. You have to educate yourself and seek out help first. That bears repeating. You need to start paying attention to what is happening around you.

You need to seek out help. You need to take action and educate yourself. There is no cavalry. You learning now, here reading this book.

You're starting to pay attention. You are your own "white knight".

Let this book be part of the arsenal that you use to save yourself and your family.

Rewind to 2016. I'm now sitting at Jenny's kitchen table trying to help her put the pieces back together. She is now 70 and I'm trying to make sure I can do everything in my power to help her. She tells me the whole story and explains to me how she uses up all of her social security each month on what's left on the mortgage and spends the rest on food and sometimes presents for the grandchildren... Not the life she imagined for herself in 2008 when she was just about to retire...

One of the most troubling things she told me is that while the markets were in freefall, here is what her broker would tell her about her 401k…(at age 62!)

"Wait it out."

"Let it ride."

"Don't worry – your portfolio is safe."

"Remember, you're in it for the long haul."

"You're majority bonds, so don't worry."

"Stay focused, be patient."

Take your feelings out of the equation."

"Don't worry. You're diversified."

"We're still I n a bull market."

"We're not at the peak yet."

"Now's not the time to take your money out."

"You will always recover."

And so on…

I know you have heard this from financial advisors before, maybe in 2008 or maybe now? These phrases are overused and very common. These "cookie-cutter" statements are what some advisors tell their clients to "keep them put" in the market. Why would they want you to stay in the market? This is the way most advisors get paid…It's called Assets Under

Management or AUM, which we will get into in the next chapter.

These are the same statements you heard from large banks and financial institutions right before the crash of 2008. "Well, David, didn't the market come back stronger than ever since then?"

Yes, yes it did. But for the people who were about to retire in 2008 it was devastating. Not only did they lose savings, they lost the lifetime income potential those savings could have provided as well. The lucky ones who had other sources of income had to wait until around 2016 to get back everything they'd lost, not including homes lost and most important of all TIME lost.

Here is the truth:

During my time as an agent/advisor in this financial and insurance industry over the years, there have been countless "Jenny's". Countless people, married, single, divorced…all Jenny's that just never really paid attention and made sure they had safeguards on their retirement accounts. They just didn't know any better. It was the same story over and over and over again, and all I could do was try my best to do as much as I could to help them put the pieces back together. Trust me – I helped them save money on health insurance costs, future medical costs, and helped them safeguard what they had. But boy, could they have been in a different place if they'd paid attention or met someone like me sooner.

If only these Jenny's knew there was another way and were educated on different retirement account options. Retirement accounts with less risk. No more ifs, maybes or shoulda, coulda, wouldas.

I need your commitment to pay attention.

Fast forward to today, the year 2020. It's been over 10 years and it has been my personal mission to find the best strategies to protect my clients like I would protect my own family. Strategies for all 3 retirement needs that the majority of my clients need: Safety, Growth and Guaranteed Lifetime Income.

Are you a Jenny? Are you not paying attention to your retirement accounts? Are you retiring soon or already retired? Is your Broker/Advisor telling you to "Stay put" as the perfect economic storm is brewing?

As I type this today, the economy has officially been in a recession since February of this year 2020; the world is going through a health pandemic with COVID 19; 40 million+ people are unemployed; and there is social, socioeconomic and racial unrest around the world. The markets recently dropped 35%, and our political leaders are dividing up the country for their own corporate sponsored agendas.

And then there is you. You and your family, who are doing the best you can to stay healthy and just try to make it work, live a happy life and make sure your family is protected.

The time is NOW to pay attention. The time is NOW to pay attention.

You can't afford to be just another Jenny.

Pay attention.

The Next Market Crash

According to Forbes, CNBC, Fox Business and countless other publications before the market recession this year, the past 11 years have been the longest bull market (up market) in U.S. history.

According to Forbes columnist, James Burman, "The markets are dangerously overvalued and we're at the peak, heading towards a crisis we've never seen before."

We've already started in this trend. We are currently technically in a recession as of the time of this writing.

Famed economist Ted Bauman predicted the collapse of the dot-com bubble and crash of 2008. Bauman now warns: "There are 3 key economic indicators that would lead to a 70% market collapse."

In simple terms:

1. The increasing market price-to-earnings ratio, which then leads to…

2. Herd mentality pullback, based on unjustifiable pricing, and…

3. Large cap stocks out performing short cap stocks.

Short cap stocks are usually an indication of where the economy is now — a "confidence" of now. A large cap stock is purchased for the long-term hold, indicating the need for safety.

According to Joseph Hargett of Yahoo Finance, if Bauman predicts a 70% market correction, one should pay very close attention.

Now pay very close attention, because what I'm about to share with you may very well change the way you feel about the risk you are currently taking in your retirement plans.

I want to be very clear: "letting it ride" is not a strategy for someone nearing or in retirement. I repeat. The advice of "letting it ride "may not be the best strategy for someone at retirement age at this point in the economic cycle.

If you are nearing retirement, you are no longer contributing to your accounts. You are taking funds out of your accounts, so if you need those funds to live on, pay close attention. When nearing retirement or in the distribution phase and you need income from your accounts, "letting it ride" is a mathematical mistake.

If you can be placed in a better situation with guarantees of principal protection, no risk of loss, no management fees and a reasonable rate of return that beats inflation, your income will last you a longer period of time. We will dive deeper into how this is possible in the coming chapters.

"We are only as blind as we want to be"

Maya Angelou

CHAPTER 2

HOW MOST BROKERS ARE PAID

L et's talk about how most financial advisors are paid. If the stock market is the casino, financial advisors are the card dealers —friendly faces dealing you options that all end up being for the benefit of the casino owner, not you, the gambler.

Now I am not saying this is true for every advisor. There are good ones and bad ones, and I'm sure by now you have dealt with both. When an advisor pushes only market-based accounts regardless of your age, timeline or what is suitable for you, this may be due to how they are being compensated. It doesn't matter if your accounts are up or down. Year after year, like clockwork, there is a slow transfer of retirement wealth going on from Main Street to Wall Street – and it's not your fault.

The problem is that most advisors still have you in the market at your age, not based on what is suitable for you, but based on the fees that they get for keeping your money in the market; where your retirement savings are at the whim of external factors like trade wars, interest rate hikes, low interest rates, political games, government shutdowns, future global viruses, social and racial unrest… and the list goes on and on.

This problem is also the reason why there are large transfers of wealth from retirement accounts to financial advisors year after year that have cost the American retiree billions in fees.

According to the National Association of Retirement Plan Participants, more than half of American workers don't even realize they're paying fees on their retirement accounts. This group collectively paid over $35 billion dollars in fees in 2018.

Even worse, these totally legal fees taken from your accounts occur regardless if the market goes up or down, and some fees don't have to be itemized on your statements. They just come out of your principal like magic – poof! Gone. Just like that.

So what exactly is the problem with **putting ALL of your hard-earned retirement funds into a managed brokerage account?**

The problem is you're paying someone 1-3% from your retirement savings year after year, for them to put your money at risk in the market. **They aren't the ones taking on any risk. YOU ARE…**

Retirees and pre-retirees, I need you to understand this… **YOU are paying someone else to risk your money in volatile markets, with no guarantees and no safety net,**

when you most likely want or need to live off of this money for the REST OF YOUR LIFE...

David F. Swensen, Chief investment officer at Yale University since 1985, has slammed many financial companies for charging excessive fees and not living up to their fiduciary responsibility.

That's like paying a fee to a casino to let the casino gamble for you, lose your money – and you *still* pay them fees!...There is no control in that. We are going to dig deeper, moving forward, and I'm going to tell you how to get your control and independence back. But first I need to continue to educate you on a few more factors so you can fully understand the problems we all face in retirement.

By the end of this book I am going to share how you can simply reallocate your retirement today to safely grow your retirement savings tomorrow, eliminate market loss, and eliminate the recurring fees you're being charged. That may sound like a fantasy to many of you reading this, but I assure you it's a fact that many retirees are living today and you're about to learn about it. A stress-free, no-drama, zero-market-risk, zero-fees, lifetime-income reality. Yes. I said zero-market loss.

In the crash of 2008, most people lost 40-50% of their retirement savings. Here's the good news: this isn't going to be you this time. You are not going to be a "Jenny". (Sorry for using your name so much, Jenny, but you share the story of so many retirees).

Let other people gamble their retirement away in the next crash. Let them accept the outdated advice from their advisors whom they overpay for doing literally nothing. Let them feel out of control. Let them worry, and let them be cheated by Wall Street. Let them "ride it out." Let them be Jenny's.

Not you. Not this time. You have a way out.

You can have the retirement of your dreams. You don't have to worry about having enough income in retirement or your money lasting. You don't have to worry about losing your life savings in the next market crash. You can follow a proven method that will preserve 100% of your retirement principal.

I know you may be thinking this sounds too good to be true... But don't just take it from me. According to the greatest investor of all time on CNBC's show 'On the Money', Warren Buffett specifically recommends this type of strategy as a way to boost retirement savings, stating "I think it's the thing that makes the most sense practically all of the time."

This system will work if you are just planning your retirement or have been retired for years.

Lack of Control

What goes into the advice that fee-based financial planners are offering today are the same underlying problems of why people were led to lose 40% of their retirement savings in 2008 and 35% recently in 2020.

The rules changed along the way and nobody told you. The fact is that financial advisors can give a retiree advice to stay in the market instead of doing what's right and suitable for their clients. In fact, many of their strategies and tactics you might be using today could actually be hurting you, not helping you.

In this book I am going to tackle the current problems and symptoms of Wall Street as they relate to the next market crash, and tell you exactly what you can do to get inflation-beating average returns, regardless of any downturns in the market, while completely eliminating market risk and fees.

In this book I am going to reveal to you a proven method called the **Retirement Rescue System** that makes this possible. I will explain it in good old plain English so it's not confusing and not filled with financial jargon, double talk or mumbo jumbo.

In 2020, chances are if you've been in the market for the past 11 years you're riding a bit high due to inflated market gains. But now **you've taken a big loss recently and you're currently telling yourself you're waiting for the market to come back or drop again before making any moves**... Wait – are *you* telling yourself that or did your broker tell you to do that...**Hmm? Are you paying attention? Jenny?**

Whatever goes up must come down. And when you're in retirement and it's down, that jeopardizes your long-term income. Jeopardizing your long-term income jeopardizes your health, your freedom, your ability to live life, your ability to give back, your ability to be the best you can be in retirement. This feeling of running out of money or not having enough is the worst feeling. The anxiety, the sleepless nights, the frantic phone calls to your advisor only to hear them try and calm you down, and you settling on riding it out based on them speaking financial jargon(at you) and you saying *okay*...You know this is how it goes. Denial isn't just a river in Africa. Kidding, but you know what I mean. You've heard this before. When you know you only have a certain amount of money at retirement and you're trying to make it last and you see the news about [*insert anything bad*], you get that worry, that awkward twinge in the pit of your stomach that tells you something just isn't right when that market roller coaster begins to descend again and again. Why put yourself through that if you don't have to?

I'll show you that you truly don't have to.

American Billionaire Financier Carl Icon recently stated, "Today's markets look like a casino on steroids."

If you've experienced one of these symptoms you understand the feelings that gambling in the stock market can cause. I call this phenomenon the "I-don't-even-want-to-see-my-statement" feeling. You know... the nausea you get when you even get a statement in the mail. It's your brain wanting to avoid pain. You see it in the pile, you pretend it's not there, then you slip it in a kitchen drawer somewhere in the hopes it will go away. You are not alone. Every Jenny does this. I mean, *everybody* does this. You need to open those up and read them.

Pay attention.

We've seen a downturn in 2020.We are currently, technically in a recession. We are in a health crisis with 40 million+ Americans are out of work. And so on. Let's be hopeful about the direction of our world. But let's be realistic about your retirement timeline.

"Stop trying to keep up with the joneses, they're broke"

-Dave Ramsey

CHAPTER 3

AMERICA'S RETIREMENT EPIDEMIC

Jenny (from our example earlier) is not the only one who is going through the wringer in retirement. 50 million Americans are going to retire over the next few years, and a lot of people are dead broke and living on credit. Even if they don't look like it...Even if your neighbors making $100k+, they are most likely spending $150k+ and have little saved. This is a statistical fact.

They're broke. They just have a socially graceful way of hiding it.

Yup. That's the majority of Americans.

Understand that most of the populations entering into retirement do not have enough saved to last even a 10-year period. More alarming, according to recent statistics, 69.8% of Americans have less than $1,000 saved for an emergency. 70%! Jesus, Mary and Joseph! That's the majority of people. But hopefully that isn't you. You've done well for yourself. You're reading a book about retirement strategies, so hopefully you have more than a thousand bucks saved.

If you are one of the lucky few with a healthy retirement and pension, safeguarding your future and income should be your biggest priority.

People are worried about their pension, social security and relying on their children to help them in retirement.

Because money-depleting factors are inescapable (which we will discuss in the next chapter), baby boomer savings have dwindled. Without a basic fundamental understanding of how we got here and the will to educate yourself on different options, life as you know it can go south in a very short period of time.

How did this all get started?

The effects of the 2020 health and economic crisis have touched everyone. Even if you have a good job and a paid-up mortgage, chances are your monthly 401k will remind you that you're always at risk of losing a good chunk of your savings in a short period of time.

In 2020, trillions of dollars evaporated from 401k accounts that had been the prime source of retirement funds for a majority of American workers, affecting their psyche and their future.

If you're still young enough, there's time to rebuild and recover and in later works I will teach you how you can accomplish a tax-free retirement. But if you're in your 50s, 60s or beyond, the consequences can be dire, and it's drawing attention to the shortcomings of the retirement systems that jeopardize the financial wellbeing of millions of people. What type of retirement vehicle allows people to lose 40-50% of their life savings just as they near retirement? **A retirement vehicle that was never designed for retirement distributions. The 401k.**

Pay attention.

Your retirement account of choice: The 401k

David Ray, President of the profit-sharing 401kCouncil of America and a lobbyist for the 401k industry, was interviewed after the collapse of 2008 and said, "The 401k empowers people to make their own investment decisions" and, "The 401k is the absolute best way people can save for retirement, absolutely the best retirement vehicle we have." He was then asked, "What about the millions of retirees who have lost their life savings?"

"That's not a 401k problem, that's an entire investment system problem."

He goes on to say, "Everyone had multiple investment options including low-yield guaranteed returns."And he believes that if you have lost money in the market, that you have "no one to blame but yourself."

He goes on to say: "In America, our society is based on freedom of choice and personal responsibility. We need to help them understand these responsibilities and execute them the best they can for one. There is no guarantee."

… And right there lays the biggest problem you face in your retirement accounts right now…that quote from the president of the 401k Council. "There are no guarantees."

The interviewer went on to ask, "What about the people who are 63 or 64? Millions of these people were thinking about retiring; now they have to go back to the workforce…"

He smiled and said, "Well, but that's not a 401k problem, that's an investment system problem, and markets go up and down. And if those people chose to take equity risk, then that was their outcome."

Two major points that I want you to take away from this interview based on your current plans… "Investment system problem" and "There are no guarantees."

In fact, the 401k plans that have become the primary source of retirement income for 60 million Americans were never designed to be retirement plans in the first place.

According to Richard Angle of Time Magazine from the cover story "Time to Retire the 401k", after researching the source of the 401k and how it has evolved to be most Americans only source of retirement money today, problem plaguing millions and millions of American retirees from the last crisis in 2008 to the 2020 recession is that most people are unaware that

the 401k as a financial vehicle was created by Congress as a tax loophole for executives 30 years ago. It was never meant to be the primary vehicle for retirement, but over the last 20 years it has become just that for ordinary Americans.

After the 401k became a way for Wall Street to gather massive amounts of money from workers, the 401k became available to average everyday employees. They then began to grow in popularity. The 401k plan would act as a savings plan and tax-deferred shelter for ordinary Americans. Sounds good, right? The idea was that employers would match a portion of the contributions, and taxes would be deferred until the employee reached the age of 59½.

It was supposed to supplement the two traditional income streams for retirees, Social Security and pensions —one leg of a three-legged stool that would support American workers into their golden years, but it didn't turn out that way.

It turned out that for the corporations that originally had to provide pensions for their employees; the 401k alternative became so much more appealing as 401ks turned out to be so much cheaper than funding pensions. Companies then decided to freeze their pension plans and replace them with 401ks. The decision sparked the creation of millions of new employee "investors" for Wall Street, and they pounced on the opportunity. This is when mutual-fund companies were created.

As you read in the previous chapter, this wealth transfer of fees has reached approximately $35 billion a year that are transferred from regular 401k investors like you to line the pockets of Wall Street. And you allow it to happen year in and year out because everyone does it without question, and that's "just the way it is". (Insert boiling frog in water analogy here).

When employers began to use 401ks as retirement plans, Wall Street did not hold back on promoting them as the best new shiny tool, and the prospect of trillions of dollars in the hands of unsophisticated investors opened the door for all sorts of abuses that eventually led to the collapse of the markets in 2008.

The fact is that the average 401k "investor" is a financial novice and they are given a list of 20-30 mutual funds to choose from with powerful sounding names with dozens of hidden fees, and these fees aren't at all transparent. It's estimated that over a 30-year period these fees can eat up half the income in some 401k plans. Investors have tried to make provisions, but the politicians that profit from the status quo and the 401k lobbies are too powerful.

I know what you're thinking: "Geez, if I knew this book was all doom and gloom I wouldn't have picked it up!" Don't worry – you're almost at the good part, the so-now-what part, the reason-you-bought-this-book part. Understand that it's important for you as a consumer to take a sober look at the reality around you today. Knowing where you are prepares you to set your sails for where you want to go.

"College graduates spend 16 years gaining skills that will help them command a higher salary; yet little or no time is spent teaching them to save, invest and grow their money"

-Vince Shorb, CEO of the National Financial Educators Council

CHAPTER 4

MONEY-DEPLETING FACTORS & EDUCATION

This may sound dramatic, but your world is being eaten away slowly right in front of you. There is an eroding force at work that is after you, your family and everyone you love. The government, financial institutions and corporations are after every penny you have. They do it by legislation, taxes, fees, inflation, and much more. Think I'm kidding? Here are some of the money-depleting factors below.

The Governments use federal and state taxes, local income taxes, capital gains tax, social security tax, real estate tax, devaluation of money, Medicare/Medicaid, Estate & Inheritance Tax.

Financial Institutions use fees, charges, penalties, commissions, market fluctuations, built-in risks, credit cards, loan interest, premiums, bad advice, bad products, and low bank rates.

Corporations use inflation, planned obsolescence, technological changes, hidden persuasion, pricing, packaging, expirations, add-ons, service calls.

It is up to YOU to pay attention to the game, your life and your money. It is up to YOU to search out ways to limit this consistent barrage of these money-depleting factors. They are coming for your hard-earned dollars, and they don't discriminate.

"Life is rigged against the financially uneducated,

So pay attention."

We weren't taught this in school. Not only were we not taught the more complex topics like how to safeguard our lives from the money-depleting factors that bombard us every day, we weren't taught even simple personal finance skills like budgeting, saving, compound interest and investing. These must be self-taught.

In fact, doing some research, I found that ultimately the school system as we know it today was created around 1902 with a big influence by John D. Rockefeller who created the General Education Board. What they did was they created a system where schools would be in the business of turning out employees. At that time factory workers weren't complete sheep, but weren't taught financial literacy (to think outside the box). This continues in some fashion today.

Therefore learning, especially financial education, can't stop after school, but rather needs to be a lifelong journey…or in my case, an obsession.

This is why it's so critical to immerse yourself in this learning to improve your financial education. You need to pull information from different sources and hold yourself accountable to learn as much as you can about bettering your financial situation.

You must understand there are options outside of the typical market-based, risk-based retirement plans. You need to hold yourself accountable for what you put into your mind, or you'll end up settling for less or being left behind in life.

Let this book help you put the pieces together while on your journey of understanding. It's up to you to learn how to set yourself up for retirement and how to invest in assets that are going to hedge against inflation. It's up to you to allocate towards safe and solid investments for your retirement income.

Learn to budget and run your personal finances just like a business, otherwise you'll find yourself "out of business" and at the full force of these money-depleting factors mentioned above.

You have to take responsibility and hold yourself accountable, because you cannot count on school systems, government, religion, politics or osmosis via couch surfing Netflix to educate yourself based on what your specific financial needs are. Only you can do that.

We all wish we had more time and freedom to do what we want and what we love. However, it is only in the real-life application of one's specialized knowledge and applied financial education that one can obtain real freedom —*time freedom*.

Let this book be your claim to that responsibility. Let this book be the wind in your sail when you boldly declare...

"I am the master of my fate,

I am the captain of my soul."

– William Ernest Henley

"Inflation is one form of taxation that can be imposed

Without legislation"

-Milton Friedman

CHAPTER 5

THE SLOW EROSION OF INFLATION

Having a healthy savings or liquid funds in the bank for emergencies is important. Having instant access to cash when you need it should always be part of your financial plan. On average, it's a rule of thumb to keep around 6-12 months of expenses available for emergencies, depending on how many dependents you have.

When you get to that phase in life where you have enough saved, you start to think about what else you can do with those funds instead of letting them "collect dust" in savings. You might then begin to look at your bank's CDs (Certificate of Deposits).CDs are short-term financial products sold by banks and credit unions. They offer a fixed interest growth in exchange for the bank using your funds for a set period of time, usually 3 to 6 months or 1 to 5 years, depending on the CD's maturity date of choice. The more money you place in a CD and the longer your CD's term, the higher the interest rate the bank will give you.

In a low-rate environment like today, bank rates are so low they are pretty much useless. There was a time when CDs were paying 16%. The highest CD rate to date was October of 1981 at 16.691%. Its lowest rate to date was in May of 2010 at 0.278%.

We are no longer rewarded for access savings. We live in a debt-based economy now where bank rates are low, money is cheap, and savers are not rewarded for keeping money in the bank. We are now rewarded for taking on debt so we can be in a perpetual debt interest-payment cycle, paying those profiting from the wealth-depleting factors.

So why do we want to keep all our money in banks if they aren't paying? Convenience, ignorance and a social construct of the banks' safety. You can only do what you know.

The problem is inflation

What is inflation? In a nutshell, inflation is the general increase in prices, goods and services each year. Meaning if your investments don't grow over the inflation rate, your money is losing future buying power.

This is important. Pay attention.

According to bankrates.com, today's CD rates are paying around 1% to 2% for 1-5-year terms. The problem with that is inflation. Inflation fluctuates, but has been hovering around 2% for the past several years.

This means that if you are not making any growth on your savings, then you are actually losing money or the purchasing power of those dollars every year due to inflation. And if you are making 2-3% on your money, you are just breaking even with inflation, and no real growth is occurring.

Let me explain it again. Banks are offering little to nothing when it comes to interest earned. CDs are, at average, 1-2%. This is close to nothing, and when you factor in inflation, it's actually less than nothing!

Here is an easy example.

If inflation is roughly 2% annually and your funds are making 0%, in reality it's actually a 2% **loss** every year.

If inflation is roughly 2% annually and your funds are making 2% on a bank CD there is +0% real growth happening. Get it?

Funds that are collecting dust instead of interest are losing future purchasing power due to inflation.

So if you are looking for safety and growth in retirement, you may have the safety at the bank, but you definitely can do better when it comes to the growth. I'm going to show you a way you can have both the safety *and* the growth you have been looking for.

It's always good to re-read something if you don't understand. If you don't understand that inflation is slowly eating away at your savings, then please re-read this chapter until it clicks, because we are about to get into the solution here shortly.

By now you should have an understanding of the problems pre-retirees and retirees like yourself are facing: the lack of financial education; the lack of control most investments have; the risk you are taking and the fees you are paying; the importance of paying attention; what money-depleting factors are eating away at your hard-earned money; and where we are right now in the economic cycle.

"Retirement is like a long vacation in Las Vegas. The goal is to enjoy it the fullest, but not so fully that you run out of money."

– Jonathan Clements

PART 2

UNDERSTANDING THE SOLUTION

"Rule No.1: Never lose money.

Rule No.2: See Rule No.1."

– Warren Buffett

CHAPTER 6

THE "POWER OF ZERO" LOSS IN RETIREMENT

The talking heads on cable TV shows would have you believe that if you gather the right information quickly enough or time the market just right, you'll somehow turn your retirement dollars into a never-ending income stream.

While chasing the next big thing in a 24-hour news cycle may seem exciting to some, it seldom works for the average investor who simply wants to make sure they have enough principal and growth in their accounts to live on in retirement.

As the President of a financial and insurance services firm, I've found that the real key to making money for my clients in retirement isn't chasing the stock market – it's "the power of zero". I don't mean zero growth; I mean the power of never taking a loss in retirement. The power of zero is the power of zero losses.

The power of never taking a loss on down-market years might sound like fiction. We've been wired to believe that to have sufficient growth, we must take more risk. This is a thought process that is difficult to let go. One of the false long-held beliefs I repeatedly come across is the either/or mind trap when it comes to risk-versus-reward for retirement savings. When nearing or in retirement, many people believe they only have two options:

Option 1: Keeping their funds safe in a CD or savings account and settling for the low interest rates banks offer that currently do not keep up with inflation.

Option 2: Keeping funds at risk in the market to make returns that beat inflation, and hopefully having enough to live on.

But these aren't the only options. Over the years, the marketplace has given birth to new financial vehicles that have fundamentally changed the way we look at risk-versus-reward in retirement income planning.

It's very satisfying to take a problem we thought difficult and find a simple solution. The best solutions are always simple

- Ivan Sutherland

CHAPTER 7

THE SOLUTION– SAFETY, GROWTH AND INCOME

I believe the key to making a solid inflation-beating return in retirement isn't in taking big risks with your hard-earned nest egg, but in eliminating potential losses entirely. Earning market-like returns while at the same time eliminating any loss of principal can help make your money last in retirement. "Well," you're thinking, "who offers that?"

These strategies exist in vehicles that are provided by insurance companies. These vehicles index or mirror the market's growth only, and when the market corrects or crashes, your principal and growth are locked in and stay intact.

This is possible through a Fixed Index Annuity. A Fixed Index Annuity is a retirement vehicle which allows you to participate in the growth of an index such as (for example, S&P 500 or NASDAQ Composite) and a list of others.

You are able to participate in the growth of the market, but without the risk of losing your principal. These policies include a no-loss guarantee that protects your funds from market loss and allows you to receive lifetime income. Yes, lifetime income means income until you die, and any remaining account value goes to your beneficiaries…and yes, this exists.

Don't let the word "indexed" fool you. Your funds are never actually in the market. They are in an account that is mirroring the growth of the market, and only the growth, which is then credited to your principal every policy year.

However, if the market goes down, your money is safe and protected from loss. The rate of return is called your participation rate. Your participation rate is the rate that you, the policy owner, get to keep as growth is credited to your account. You are trading a participation rate for never having a loss in the market. Some Fixed Index Annuities have participation rates of over 100%!

Here are two hypothetical examples of how a Fixed Index Annuity using a No Cap S&P 500 point-to-point allocation strategy would be credited.

Example 1: If your participation rate was 85% and the S&P 500 went up 10%, your principal would be credited and locked in at 8.5%!

Example 2: If the S&P 500 goes down 40%, like in 2008, you lose nothing, and your principal is intact!

Here is a chart that is easy to follow:

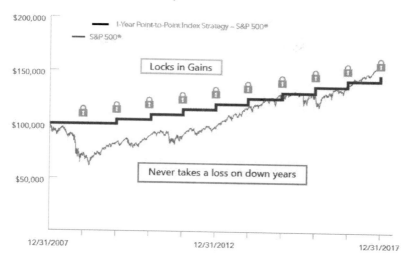

Each policy year, any interest credits earned are locked in. Even if the market goes down, the growth already received will not be lost. This is what a basic Fixed Index Annuity looks like.

In addition, you can rollover your qualified or non-qualified funds into a Fixed Index Annuity. This is a simple, non-taxable transfer.

When shopping for annuities, make sure you review and understand the surrender charges involved, any fees on the policy, including rider fees and allocation fees, if any. Make sure you understand how the participation rates and all of the above-mentioned details affect your annuity.

Make sure you understand the type of annuity that best fits your specific needs, age and timeline, based on your specific situation, before making your decision. Annuities are complex, so make sure you have a financial or insurance professional go through all the details, pros and cons, based on your specific needs for safety, growth and income.

"It's what you learn after you know it all that counts"

–Harry S Truman

CHAPTER 8

THE RRS METHOD & THE BENEFITS

The Retirement Rescue System (RRS) Method uses vehicles that are independent of any stock market risk to provide growth, guarantees of principal protection and lifetime income.

Fixed Index Annuity: Benefits

I. Principal Growth Without Loss

In a Fixed Index Annuity you get the upside Index growth potential, with zero market risk.

For some, market-like returns with no risk of loss sounds like a fantasy. When introducing this option to first-timers I sometimes get a, "Aha! Hmm…Yeah, that doesn't sound right!" or "That sounds too good to be true!"

Fortunately for you it's not a fantasy. It's a reality.

Your funds are in an account that is indexed or mirrored to the market's growth – and only the growth. The insurance companies that offer these policies credit your principal each year based on the growth of the index your Fixed Index Annuity is mirroring.

Again, your funds are not actually in the market. They are in an account that is mirroring the index growth and being credited on an annual basis and when the market goes down, your account stays level, you lose zero. This is where the term "Zero is hero" was coined. No risk of loss is the power of zero. That is extremely powerful.

If you are thinking: "How do the insurance companies make money?" Your funds in a Fixed Index Annuity are actually being invested by the insurance company.

I'll use a bank analogy to make it easy to understand the concept.

Say you have $100k and you walk into your local bank. You tell the teller you want to open a savings account. The teller then takes your $100k and funds your account. You walk out with a smile on your face. You go back to the bank the next day and ask the teller to see your funds.

The teller turns the screen around and says, "See, there's your $100k", meaning your $100k isn't sitting in a vault in the back of the bank waiting for you to come get it. It's being lent out by the bank for interest. Your bank uses your money to make them money and gives you nothing in return. Insurance companies do the same thing except they usually put the funds in bonds that provide downside protection and options that have upside gains, but regardless, when you need your money, it's there. Does that make sense?

If not, just know that these accounts aren't magic trickery, but rather a predictable set of formulas that actuaries (math geniuses) prepare for insurance companies to have the best chance of making more money for themselves than they pay out over time.

None of your funds are actually invested in the particular market your Fixed Index Annuity is tracking, and that's why you have no actual market risk.

Based on your funds having no risk of loss and being credited based on market index growth, you have a better chance of your funds growing in a more effective way. When looking to take critical income from your retirement accounts over time, even small increases make a HUGE difference.

For instance, let's take the **Rule of 72**. If you are only earning a 3% return, it would take 24 years for your money to double. Make an average 4%, and your money doubles in 18 years. If you can average 6%, your money would double in 12 years and quadruple in 24 years. When you're taking upside gains without losses, these 4-6% averages are possible. Some indexed allocations have 8% averages without caps. This is game changing to understand.

II. No Fees

Most Fixed Index Annuities have no contract or management fees. The mathematical benefit for not having any fees is a huge deal for any retiree. The fact that you don't have to pay to own and operate an account that gets market-like returns is a game changer. When you eliminate risk and eliminate fees from your retirement accounts, your accounts last longer in general.

For example, if you have a brokerage account with $300k that has 2% annual fees (not including growth or any other factors), this is how this plays out over a 10-20-year period. 2% of $300k is $6,000 per year. Multiply that by 10 years and that is $60k in fees. Multiply that by 20 and that's $120k in fees. Each year these fees take away from your growth over time.

The fact that most Fixed Index Annuities have no fees is a beautiful thing. So you may be thinking, "How does my agent make money? They have to make something. They aren't working for free." Yes, the agents who offer Fixed Index Annuities are making a commission, but none of that commission gets taken from your principal.

It's important to note **while your agent does make a commission, it does NOT come out of your principal. Their commission gets paid directly from the Insurance Company's reserves.**

III. The Bonus

Most of these rated companies are in such high competition with each other for your business that they sometimes offer what is known as **the bonus**. The bonus can come in many different forms, but the most common form is a benefit-based or income-based bonus.

The income-based bonus is a bonus that is added to the principal amount that you transfer into your annuity.

For example, if the insurance company offering the Fixed Index Annuity was offering new policy holders a 20% bonus, that means that if you were to transfer $100,000 into the new Fixed Index Annuity Policy, the contract would credit your income base $20,000. So your income base for your policy would start out at $120,000. 20% of $100k is $20k.20% of $200k is $40k, and so on and so forth.

As you can see, the power of having a bonus feature on your money is so amazing, because it allows you to achieve an upgraded value in your retirement immediately.

Most of these bonuses are credited upon transfer, so that means that you have 20% more in income from your retirement account. Also important to note, most of these bonuses are not principal bonuses, meaning the funds are not added to your principal. They are added to what's called the income base.

The income base is where your lifetime income will be drawn from, but nonetheless, these are powerful tools, powerful features to have on your account to be able to instantly increase your retirement income.

IV. Tax-Deferred Growth– Triple Compound Growth

Let's talk about tax-deferred growth and what that means. Tax-deferred growth means that you do not pay tax on an annual basis for the growth of your annuity. The tax on the growth is deferred, similarly to your 401k growth or your IRA growth. These are examples of tax-deferred accounts. Tax-deferred growth allows your account to have what is called "triple compound growth" – meaning, growth on your principal, growth on your interest and growth on the taxes you otherwise would have paid. So when you are deferring tax on an annual basis on your growth account, this allows you not have to worry about receiving a 1099 at the end of the year, because you don't have to pay tax on the growth of your Fixed Index Annuity.

If your Fixed Indexed Annuity is funded by qualified funds (funds from IRA, 401k, tax-deferred money), once you start taking income from this account, the income will be taxable.

If your FIA is funded by Non-Qualified finds (cash, CD, savings, etc.), your funds will still grow tax-deferred, but the original principal will never be taxed as it has already been taxed prior to placement into the annuity. The taxable income when taking withdrawals will be on the interest gained only.

That money taken out would be taxed as income. If you fund your annuity with non-qualified funds, meaning cash CD money, savings, etc., you would never pay tax on that original amount because you've already paid tax on that cash. With an annuity that is funded with non-qualified funds, you're only paying tax on the growth when you take money out of the annuity for income.

Your annuity still grows tax-deferred, but you're paying tax only on the growth when you're taking money out for income. So let's go over that again because I think it's important that you understand there are two types of money in retirement: qualified money and non-qualified money.

Qualified money is money that is coming from your 401k or IRA or your qualified retirement accounts. Money that you've been deferring tax on for your entire working life — that's called qualified money.

Non-qualified money is money that is coming from bank savings, checking, CD money — money that you've already paid tax on. Get it? So when we're talking about retirement funds, we're always talking about two types of money: qualified money and non-qualified money. Think of it this way: 401k or IRA money is qualified; cash is non-qualified money. Got it? Okay. Let's move on.

V. Index Allocation options – Laddering strategies

Okay. So we're going to discuss index allocation options for your Fixed Index Annuity. Now each Fixed Index Annuity contract is going to offer you different indexing allocation options with the most popular index being the S&P 500. With that being said, you have multiple options for your indexing strategies.

The insurance company is going to give you a list of choices, and your financial professional should guide you through the difference between those indices. They should know which index that contract has to offer will give you the biggest growth rate.

There's an average growth rate for each index and you want to be able to go with the one that has the highest growth, whether it be the S&P 500 that they're mirroring or whether it be Barclays Trailblazer index or NASDAQ index. There's a litany of index choices that you can choose from.

There are two-year point-to-point strategies, one-year point-to-point strategies, and month-to-month average strategies, but regardless, you're given options in regard to index strategies, and this is what allows you to be able to get market-like returns on your Fixed Index Annuity, because you are mirroring the indices growth. In other words, you are mirroring the market's growth without the risk.

Laddering strategies

Laddering strategies or combining 2 or more index strategies within the allocations of a Fixed Index Annuity – this simply means that you are parsing your strategy and using multiple indexes.

So locking in the annual growth with ladder-allocation strategies unlocks the growth potential of a Fixed Index Annuity. These strategies determine how much interest will be credited to your account that year.

They also determine how often interest credits are received. A two-year crediting strategy generally offers higher crediting rates than a 1-year strategy powered by the same index.

So just like laddering a few CDs together, you can ladder the allocation options within your single Fixed Index Annuity policy which gives you an overall diversity in multiple indexes.

VI. No-Cap Index Option

Having a No-Cap index option, if possible, is incredibly powerful. Imagine you have 2 accounts. One account has a 5% cap rate on your index, which means if that index grows by 10%, you're only going to be credited 5%, because your cap rate is 5%.

Now imagine the other account has no cap on the index. That means if the index goes up 10%, you're being credited that full index growth of 10%. Better, right? This is if your participation rate is 100% participation.

You should always know what your participation rate is on your specific index choice. Having a no-cap rate or no-cap on your index allocation option allows you to obtain market-like returns.

And again, without any risk of loss, because your Fixed Index Annuity has a 0% floor which allows you not to lose a penny if the market goes down. That is wonderful.

VII. Retirement Insured – Safety of Principal

With a Fixed Index Annuity, your retirement is insured by that specific insurance carrier who is offering you the annuity contract. It's important to note that in and of itself, your Fixed Index Annuity is an insurance policy, an insurance policy that protects your retirement savings.

So, in essence, a Fixed Index Annuity is retirement insurance. It ensures you that you don't lose principal and growth, and guarantees you lifetime income.

When you think of money insured, most likely your mind goes to your bank where you would have the FDIC that is supposed to cover up to $250,000. Well, believe it or not, insurance companies provide even greater guarantees and safeguards than banks do.

There are two safeguards that are associated with annuities. The first safeguard is called Insurance Company Reserve. Insurance companies must have a reserve, even just to open your account or policy. This is a safety net in case the insurance company goes insolvent or something happens to the company. They must have a reserve.

Secondly, each state has what is called the Guaranty Association. Now the Guaranty Association is State funds that back-up the premium within your insurance policy. And for some reason the Department of Insurance doesn't allow agents or advisors to discuss the Guaranty Association when discussing annuities with clients. However, you should be informed and know what it is, because you need to learn about the safeguards that are associated with these types of annuities.

It's important to understand that the Guaranty Association covers the original premium in a policy, and you have an insurance company reserve that they must have in order to even open your account. It is important to understand that each state covers different amounts when it comes to what the Guaranty Association will cover.

So when you're thinking about all these protections and guarantees and features that are associated with Fixed Index Annuities, compare that to your existing 401k, IRAor brokerage accounts. What safety nets do you have associated with those accounts? That's a Big Fat Zero. You have zero guarantees when your funds are in the market.

You have zero guarantees when your funds are in a 401k or IRA, and if I can bet you one thing it's this…

*If your market-based portfolio, 401k or IRA had an insurance option that you could purchase that could safeguard your principal from losing a penny on a market downturn, YOU WOULD BUY IT. You would wait in line for days and buy it at a high cost because it would give you peace of mind.

Fortunately for you, these Fixed Index Annuities do just that, but without the fees and with more benefits. And you don't have to wait in a line.

VIII. Penalty-Free Withdrawals

Most Fixed Index Annuity companies that I know allow for a 10% annual penalty-free withdrawal, usually for the first 10 years. This means that for the first 10years of the annuity policy you can take out up to 10% per year for income.

For example: say you have $500,000 in your Fixed Index Annuity. You can start taking out $50,000 per year for the first 10 years, so that would equate to $4,166.66 per month. However, if you want to make your funds last through retirement on a lifetime level, you would want to take out a little less than that 10% max per year. You probably want to take you out closer to 5% to 6% annually for the first 10 years so you can allow your account to grow at the same time you're taking funds out. The penalty-free amount is different for every insurance company, but most allow for a 10% withdrawal, penalty-free.

This allows you to be able to have the necessary liquidity that first 10years –without being charged a fee for taking funds out of the account prematurely. It's also important to note that most of these Fixed Index Annuities have what's called a Terminal Illness Rider or a Convalescent Care Rider which states that there would be no penalty for taking as much money as you need from the account if you had a medical emergency or needed things such as nursing home care, but this would be discussed with your financial professional for them to go over the exact benefits of your specific Fixed Index Annuity policy.

IX. Guaranteed Lifetime Income

Guaranteed lifetime income can be considered the Holy Grail of features for a retiree, based on this being the number #1 concern or worry which is: not having enough money to last through retirement.

Guaranteed lifetime income itself sounds like an infomercial for the Publishers Clearing House, or a fantasy of some scratch-off lottery ticket win, but I assure you it's not. It's a very real and awesome feature on a very real retirement vehicle called the Fixed Index Annuity. The fact that the growth of these accounts is indexed to market growth is because some mistake them for a vehicle that is only used for growth. However, the fact that these have benefits such as guaranteed lifetime income makes these accounts attractive and even essential for income planning for retirement.

This feature allows one to be able to turn any retirement savings into lifetime income, whether the funds are coming from an IRA, 401k, TSP, 403B, CD, Savings, a 1035 exchange from another annuity or a life insurance cash value, etc. It allows the owner to be able to create a lifetime pension from that asset. This is a huge game changer for most people in retirement.

This is the feature that allows retirees to sleep at night. This is the feature that allows for a stress-free retirement. This is the feature that enables one to not have to even think about money in retirement if they have established an account with a guaranteed lifetime income. This is an incredibly powerful and valuable feature.

The ability to turn the amount that you've saved for retirement into a never-ending source of income that you cannot outlive is possibly the top reason to purchase a Fixed Index Annuity. Money that comes monthly, every year like clockwork without having to think about it needs to be fully appreciated. Also note that the income from your Fixed Index Annuity satisfies RMD (Required Minimum Distribution) on qualified funds.

What would that mean to you if you could turn your savings account into a guaranteed lifetime income stream? What would that mean to you to turn your brokerage account that is currently in the market at the whim of all of these external factors into a retirement vehicle that has no risk of loss guarantees, and an income that you can't outlive?

A few chapters ago I discussed the 401k and how it took over companies offering pension plans. This type of annuity has guaranteed lifetime income that takes back the power from Wall Street and put the power back into your hands and allows you to protect your house, protect your life, and protect your family, as it eliminates the money-deteriorating factors from your retirement account. Eliminate the risk, the fees, the worry, the stress of not knowing if you're going to have enough income coming in for the rest of your life based on the amount that you have saved.

If you take away nothing else from this book, understand that lifetime income is the master key to retirement —the shining light that most people want, but never knew existed. **Income guaranteed for life** is where you set your sails and never have to worry about running out of money ever again.

The Subtitle of this book is "How to Never Run Out of Money in Retirement". This is how you never run out of money in retirement.

X. Guaranteed Lifetime Income vs. Bond Income – Zero standard deviation

I wanted to add this benefit for all the stock market lovers out there and the Do-It-Yourself traders in retirement who think they know everything they need to know about making money in the markets. I wanted to go over some facts with you. Annuities lower your risk and increase your returns of your portfolio via bond replacement. For example: an income annuity functions like an AAA Bond (meaning strong guarantees) with a CCC yield (meaning higher returns) with Zero Standard Deviation (meaning no change in income fluctuation).

However, it also protects you from overspending in retirement, and gives you the safety and confidence you need to weather this and future financial storms you may face...*will* face.

So for you bond-income lovers out there: think about reallocating the percentage that you have in fixed income or bonds into income annuities that again function like AAA Bonds with CCC yields and have ZERO standard deviation.

XI. Beneficiary Benefits – Avoiding Probate

Along with a Fixed Index Annuity giving you safety growth and lifetime income, these accounts also give you the ability to have beneficiaries on your annuity policy. A beneficiary is a person, persons, institution or Corporation that you designate to leave your account to. If you die while there's money still left in your principal, the beneficiary of the annuity will receive those funds entirely.

Now there's been a misconception with these types of annuities that have been out there that we should address. What happens to the money in these accounts when the policy owner dies? I've heard clients say that they thought the insurance company kept the money. I've heard people say that the money just disappears. Let me put all that to bed right this second.

When you pass, the entire remaining principal, meaning every last penny, goes directly to your beneficiary. You can set the beneficiary to be anyone, from a family member to a spouse or child, even to an organization or charity of your choosing. These are revocable so you always have the power to change or add new beneficiaries.

Having a beneficiary on your account is important. Any asset you own that doesn't have a joint owner or beneficiary listed on the account has the risk of going through probate.

Probate is the legal process in which a will is reviewed to determine whether it's valid and authentic. This is the process for reviewing the assets of a deceased person and determining inheritors. With your funds in a Fixed Index Annuity, your beneficiaries will never have to go through that legal process. They avoid probate, and funds go directly to whoever the beneficiary is.

On a side note, I want to discuss briefly the importance of a Will and Trust, because the majority of people that I've helped over the years didn't have a Will and Trust set up but they all had assets that could go through probate. This again is from an overall lack of financial education.

Most people think its okay just to have a will written out, but that's not the case. In order to avoid a probate situation and a lengthy legal process with your beneficiaries having to pay legal fees and go through probate court, you want to make sure that you have a Will and Trust set up for all of your assets, including and especially your home or properties.

In fact, with most people I speak to, at the end of our initial financial review I make it part of their homework of items to take care of immediately.

XII. Annual Reset Provision

Another key feature or benefit of having a Fixed Index Annuity in your retirement strategy is the annual reset provision. This feature not only protects your principal, but it protects the growth as well. This allows you to be able to grow your retirement account mirroring the index growth, and every year that gain is locked in as your new principal which can never be lost. Once interest is credited to your Fixed Index Annuity it's always protected. This is the key feature to your principal's compounding growth.

These are the basic benefits and unique features of the Fixed Index Annuity. This is the "in a nutshell" version of how these features work. **While it is my intention to give you insight into its powerful benefits, reviewing with an insurance or financial professional is a must.**

"When the world changes around you and when it changes against you, what used to be a tail wind is now a head wind - you have to lean into that and figure out what to do because complaining isn't a strategy"

- Jeff Bezos

CHAPTER 9

A 21ST CENTURY STRATEGY FOR THE NEW NORMAL

Retirement strategies for the 21st century have to involve the safety of your principal during these rocky global economic times. At the time of this writing we are currently in a recession; there's a global pandemic health crisis with COVID-19 which is affecting the economy in a drastic way. The markets have been bullish over the last 11 years up until this year. Right now, in order for you to realize the power of zero losses in your retirement safely, securely and realistically, using a Fixed Index Annuity as part of your retirement strategy is a must. You need to be able to protect your principal from losses. You need to have access to your money, get a reasonable rate of return that hedge against inflation. A Fixed Index Annuity can do all these things. So if you're looking for a 21st century retirement plan that is up to date with what's going on. But as protection from market loss, for, regardless of anything that happens, regardless of who the President is, having an account that has reasonable rate of return and zero risk of loss and getting a guaranteed lifetime income is essential.

Let's not forget that these accounts offer you a guaranteed lifetime that you cannot outlive. That is so important for so many retirees who are going to be facing income insecurity in the future. 40 million people unemployed in the United States. Most businesses have not recovered from COVID-19. This is a turning point, at which you have to realize that we are in a new era. The New Normal of the way in which the world works. You need to be able to see and understand this, review all your options that are available to you and protect your retirement.

The Retirement Rescue System teaches you to rethink asset allocation in retirement so you can focus on safety growth and income vs. the old black-and-white models of risk vs. reward and uncertainty. Hoping for the best isn't a strategy at all.

PART 3

CONNECTING THE DOTS

"It takes as much energy to wish as it does to plan"

-Eleanor Roosevelt

CHAPTER 10

THE RRS METHOD – REVIEW, STRATEGY, EXECUTION

The Retirement Rescue System, or RRS for short, is a unique approach. When reviewing your specific situation, we have an approach that has been proven to be effective in regard to retirement planning. It's a 3-step approach:

Step 1. The first step is organization. If you don't know where you are today, how can you set your sails tomorrow? So prior to our initial meeting we will ask you to prepare a few items: your existing policies; your health insurance policies; long-term care, life insurance; financial statements such as bank CDs, money market, 401k or IRA accounts. We will review your monthly income and expenses and see where you are now. Your agent/advisor can help you organize what you have and get your files in order, to see where you are today.

After the organization process, we dig into the strategy process. We have organized your information and established what you currently have and what additional strategies you'll need to put in place, in order to reach your goals.

All the strategies we put in place must be suitable and appropriate for your specific situation.

Step 2 is Policy Review. Now that we have organized your policies and have an understanding of where you are, it's time to go through your current situation in detail. You want to make sure that you're not overpaying on your insurance and that you're not overpaying on any fees or in the account management costs. We want to make sure that your plans are in alignment with what your goals are, so when we review your policy we want to make sure everything is in alignment with where you want to be. If your current policies and accounts are not in alignment, we make sure to tailor your strategy to reach your specific goals in the most cost-effective and time-efficient way possible. Planning and execution comes into play in Step 3.

Step 3. Planning and Execution. We need to make sure your retirement make sense for today's market. So far we've organized your current accounts and policies and we've made sure that they're in alignment with what your current and future goals are, and we figured out where specific problems are hidden – and discovered one or two you may not have known existed.

Based on that current organized financial picture, we're going to go ahead and put a retirement plan together for you to see how to maximize your retirement and minimize all money-depleting factors. Again, it is crucial that you go through this process with an advisor that you can trust. Someone who you know has proven client results and credibility. Everything discussed with your agent/advisor needs to be suitable and appropriate for your specific situation. Nothing else should matter to your agent besides your satisfaction and getting results for YOU.

Understanding Your Phase

Everyone wants to make sure they have enough money to live on during retirement. In their working years, many people have some type of retirement account. It could be a 401k plan. Or, if you're a school-district employee, it could be a 403(b) or tax-sheltered annuity, a pension plan if you're a government employee or a self-directed IRA if you're self-employed. Regardless, you want to make sure you contribute as much as possible and have enough saved for your retirement years. However, the retirement timeframe is getting longer.

During your working years (also known as the "accumulation phase"), you contribute directly from your paycheck to tax-deferred accounts. This consistent contribution, regardless of market fluctuation, is called **dollar-cost averaging**. The fact that you have a good amount of time to work and contribute to your retirement accounts means you have the time and money compound to be able to sustain losses. During this phase, asset-allocation risk and growth are important.

However, in my experience working in the insurance and annuities space, the goal for most people during retirement becomes securing fixed income to make sure their money lasts for the rest of their life. The risk of loss from asset allocation in market-based accounts becomes worrisome.

When you are close to retirement or already retired, this is called the "distribution phase." The goal of this phase is to have your money last for the remainder of your life, which could be decades. So you see it's extremely important to make sure you plan to secure your fixed income over this timeframe. You must educate yourself to determine in which type of account your funds can grow and last to provide, at minimum, income for all your fixed monthly expenses and possible emergencies along the way.

The problem lies in the type of account many people are using to secure their income. If your funds are left in the same qualified market-based retirement accounts (a 401k, IRA, brokerage, etc.), your funds are at constant risk of loss, and you are knowingly or unknowingly paying a substantial amount in fees. Risk of loss and fees are the two factors that will eat into your retirement account, based on your retirement timeframe and need for income. Once you retire, you are no longer contributing to your account as you are taking constant income or withdrawals. These income needs, risk of loss and fees are what you need to factor in when rethinking your retirement allocations.

Needing consistent income and emergency funds for 20-40-plus years may be a worrisome thought to most, but it doesn't have to be. A Fixed Indexed Annuity can help you address your retirement income needs like safety of principal, guaranteed or predictable principal growth, and lifetime income.

A Fixed Index Annuity is an insurance product that allows you to get market-like returns without the risk of losing principal. It allows the policy owner to participate in a market index (such as the S&P 500), and the policy protects your funds from any market loss by giving you a no-loss guarantee. Your principal and growth are locked in every year, and if the market goes down, your principal is protected. On top of safety and tax-deferred growth, Fixed Index Annuities offer lifetime income options that allow you to receive monthly income for life, even if there is no principal in your account because of income use. Your policy will continue to pay you for your lifetime and possibly your spouse's lifetime, leaving the remaining balance to your beneficiaries.

Even though you have access to your funds along the way, one must remember that annuities are mostly long-term strategies. Canceling or surrendering an annuity before its surrender schedule timeframe can cause a surrender charge. Understanding that this type of retirement plan is a long-term strategy will eliminate the individuals this may not be suitable for. As long as you understand this, you will have a solid plan.

There are a number of insurance companies that offer annuities and even more choices in annuity contracts. It's important to choose a company with a high financial strength rating (A- or better) and that has been around for awhile. If you have questions, consider working with a financial professional whose expertise is specific to annuities. He/she can help educate you on how these accounts work and which annuity is best suited for your specific situation.

"Retirement, a time to do what you want to do, when you want to do it, where you want to do it and how you want to do it,"

– Catherine Pulsifer

CHAPTER 11

THE RRS METHOD –DEFINING YOUR IDEAL RETIREMENT

Let's make this FUN! I want you to Dream Big and we can work backwards from there. During this part of the exercise I don't want you to use any sarcasm, negativity, or pessimism to justify why your life can't be a certain way or why you can't do something.

I want you to feel free to write down all the things you want and need in your life. Write down all those goals you still haven't accomplished yet that you want to reach. What do you want the rest of your life to look like? Really feel the emotions of living the life of choice rather than current circumstance. Describe it all in great detail and write it all down. Do you want to move to Hawaii or escape to a place where the cost of living is much less? Do you want to live by the beach or off the grid? Close to family and kids? There is no wrong answer here. How do you want to live? What would you like to do every day? Do you want to commit to projects or just wonder and be free day to day? It's up to you.

Then let's see how much that would take monthly or annually for you to accomplish these dreams and goals of yours. Whether your dreams are to stay close to the kids and babysit the grandkids or fly off to new adventures... Let's see what the cost is and work backwards.

When going through this part, it's best to do it with your agent or advisor who has access to these lifetime income vehicle illustrations. Have them put some proposals together for you and see what is realistic for your income at that point.

If you're short, we can scale down and make it realistic as needed — but don't kill the dream just yet. See what you can make happen first! See what you can do! Go through this step by step and make it fun! Isn't that why you've saved for retirement anyway? To live and have some fun?!

CHAPTER 12

THE RRS METHOD – IT'S YOUR MONEY!

Some advisors make you feel that if you even *think* about doing something else with your retirement account it's like stepping into the unknown. If you tell them directly about a plan you may have researched or have in place, understand that you will for sure get the "I wouldn't do that if I were you" talk. The truth is they should be there to help YOU and make YOUR dreams as close to reality as they can be. If you aren't satisfied with your relationship with your advisor, you should seek out help. See what else other advisors have to offer and weigh your options. You should never feel stuck in your position with your current advisor. Always remember:

IT'S YOUR MONEY.

Not theirs.

"In life, as in chess, forethought wins"

- Charles Buxton

PART 4
IT'S YOUR MOVE.

"One of the greatest misconceptions about becoming successful is the idea that you should "feel good" or "motivated" before you act. Motivation always follows action, but seldom precedes it"

-George Zalucki

CHAPTER 13

YOUR ACTION PLAN

Moving forward after reading this book, you've learned that you have to start paying attention to life and what's going on with your accounts. If you don't pay attention, you know the money-depleting factors will eat away at your hard-earned money. You've learned what inflation is and the need to earn more than inflation, to reduce or eliminate fees, or else you're actually losing money.

You've learned how to grow your retirement safely without any risk of market loss. You've done more than just learn here. You've discovered that you are capable of picking up a book and learning a new way of doing something that may truly change the way you feel and reduce the anxiety you may have been living with when thinking you wouldn't have enough for your retirement years.

You should feel excited about the new possibilities that life has to offer now that you know money doesn't have to run out in retirement. Geez! What are you going to complain about now if your funds aren't affected by market downturns? I guess you'll have to focus your energy on things that matter most in life! Like family, your health, your friendships and doing whatever the heck you want to do...

You've learned to take the bull by the horns, take the power back from Wall Street's fee-sucking vampires, create the ideal retirement and work the cost backwards from your dreams to see how much income you'll need. Go through the RRS Method with a licensed professional to organize, strategize and execute your dreams and the lifetime income it will take to pay for them.

Reach out to the person who gave you this book and thank them. Schedule an appointment with them to review your retirement options. If you are currently searching for that special someone you can also reach out to us directly for additional information and education or to set up a virtual retirement strategy call.

Even though these may be tough times for our families, for the economy and for millions of people, always focus on your house first.

This is the time to reflect and really tailor your retirement.

This is the chance for you to pay attention and continue to educate yourself. The education doesn't stop with this book. This book is only one piece of your education puzzle.

Go forth with the excitement of knowing that your retirement income does not have to be dictated by Wall Street and that YOU can be IN CONTROL!

END NOTES:

Resource Guide

www.PacificUnitedFinancial.com

www.RetirementRescueSystem.com

www.TheAnnuityNerd.com

www.401kRescueSystem.com

www.CreditRescueSystem.com

Authors Contact:

David@PacificUnitedFinancial.com

ABOUT THE AUTHOR

David Abreu is an award-winning financial expert with over a decade of experience in the insurance and retirement planning industry. He is the founder and CEO of Pacific United Financial Group, a financial and insurance services firm located in San Diego, California. He has published articles with Forbes as an invite-only Forbes Finance Council Member.

David lives in San Diego with his wife Michelle and two rescue dogs, James Bond and August.

Made in the USA
Coppell, TX
03 August 2020